Five Sisters Zoo

Our Story

Text © Five Sisters Zoo
Images © Five Sisters Zoo and other copyright holders where noted

First published in 2018 by:
Glowworm Books & Gifts Ltd.
Unit 2, 5 Youngs Road, East Mains Industrial Estate,
Broxburn, West Lothian, EH52 5LY, Scotland.
Telephone: 01506 857570
http://www.glowwormbooks.co.uk

On behalf of:
Five Sisters Zoo
Gaveside, West Calder, West Lothian, EH55 8PT, Scotland.
Telephone: 01506 870000
http://www.fivesisterszoo.co.uk

ISBN 978-09557559-4-1

Printed & bound in Scotland by Airdrie Print
Design and layout by Gordon Allan
Research by Lesley Coupar

Reprint Code 10 9 8 7 6 5 4 3 2 1

This book is sold subject to the conditions that it shall not, by way of
trade or otherwise, be lent, hired out or otherwise circulated without the publishers
prior consent, in any form of binding or cover other than that in which it is
published and without a similar condition including this condition
being imposed on the subsequent purchaser.

The Story of Five Sisters Zoo

Five Sisters Zoo officially opened in 2005, but to set the scene and understand how the Zoo evolved the story begins before then for owners Shirley and Brian Curran.

For those of you who have supported the Zoo since the days of the garden centre this will be a trip down memory lane, for others visiting for the first time, we would like to share our story with you and to do this, we need to go back in time…

1993 - 2004

Brian is a landscape gardener to trade and in 1993 he and Shirley purchased 2.5 acres of land with the aim of opening a garden centre and landscaping business on a site which many years later was to become the location for the Five Sisters Zoo.

After building their new home (the only thing that hasn't changed location over the years), work began creating the new garden centre and builders yard to service the landscaping company.

With Shirley and Brian's house in the background; work begins creating a road/car park area for the garden centre.

Constructing the road and car park area for the garden centre.

The garden centre was called "The Five Sisters"- after the 5 shale bings that overlooked the new development. Locally these large hills were nicknamed the Five Sisters. Brian who is from Polbeth often used to play in and around the bings; this old photo from 1977 shows him on a motorbike with his pals. Little did he realise then what the future held for him just a short distance away!

Over the coming months and after a lot of hard work their new venture started taking shape.

Work on the new site, 3 of the shale bings in the background.

The first perimeter fence posts are put in place.

Entrance path to the garden centre under construction and the entrance taking shape.

The garden centre office during construction. This would become the café and subsequently the ticket desk and entrance.

The building was clad and the garden area designed.

Polytunnels to bring on the young plants (the only remaining original area of the garden centre, which is currently home to our lemurs).

A new pond was created. This would eventually become a home for the otters, then the pond in the walkthrough aviary.

Pathways were formed and a new summer house added.

The gardens quickly became established.

For a number of years, the garden centre and landscaping business prospered.

Aerial view of Brian and Shirley's home with the garden centre and landscaping business. The trees at the top of the photograph would eventually become part of the proposed Zoo.

A new shed was required to house indoor plants and compost etc. This in time was to become the Zoo's reptile house until it was destroyed by fire in 2013.

Another shed, nearing completion, would become a 'soft play' area, however following the fire it was destined to house The Lost Kingdom reptile centre.

Shirley and Brian are both passionate about animals and during this time were always agreeing to re-home pets that were no longer wanted or able to be looked after. They became well known for their kindness to animals and their own personal collection of animals kept on growing in numbers. Whilst parents visited the garden centre children enjoyed seeing the various animal enclosures.

2005

The collection of animals began with several rabbits, guinea pigs, goats and pigs which quickly grew to include reptiles. At this point the Council stated that if the animals were to be displayed to the public then a Zoo licence would be a mandatory requirement to ensure the necessary standards of animal welfare and public safety were met. The licence was granted in 2005. This may be regarded as the birth of the Five Sisters Zoo and the demise of the garden centre.

Using the existing infrastructure of the garden centre, enclosures were constructed and more animals started arriving. Over a period of months, the raised beds of the garden centre were adapted to become homes for meerkats, skunks, black and white ruffed lemurs and mongooses.

Some of the first animals to arrive and be homed in the new purpose built enclosures.

2007

When Edinburgh Zoo closed their reptile house, Shirley and Brian offered to re-home two West African dwarf crocodiles. The male was the first to arrive from Edinburgh Zoo and it is understood that the female had been born in the wild before being caught and sold to a private collector in England. The female was eventually removed from the private collection and was found to be in a terrible emaciated state, living in a bath and badly malnourished.

Some may remember the original crocodile house and the weekly public feeding sessions were very popular, but this house proved too hard to keep to temperature and the crocs were moved to another wooden house beside the reptile house. The pair are believed to be around 39 years old and although several eggs have been laid over the years, none have successfully fertilized.

Two ruffed lemurs – a male and female, were then acquired by the Zoo. The female fell pregnant for the first time shortly after arriving but sadly had an emergency section when in early labour and lost the babies. She successfully delivered 3 babies when she fell pregnant for the second time and it was a delight to see the family growing. Unfortunately well into her 3rd pregnancy, she had to be rushed to the Dick Vet Hospital and we sadly lost both the babies and mum. Dad is still with us (September 2017) and we hope he will be for many years to come. He's now got a new partner to keep him company.

African dwarf crocodile.

The ruffed lemur babies.

The meerkats soon settled into their new home close to the entrance – they have had a few different homes – does anyone remember this building? When the crocodiles were moved into a wooden building behind the reptile house, the old crocodile house then became the new meerkat home. The cheeky meerkats would often be running about outside of their fenced area!

The new meerkat home.

We have had many wonderful volunteers over the years, but special mention must go to Alex Oag, who, on retiring first came to the café and Zoo as a regular visitor and noticing all the "odd jobs" that needed done, in 2007 he became a volunteer 5 days a week. He was a brilliant handyman who could turn his hand to anything that needed done. He even had his own workshop at the Zoo where he could often be found fixing or building something. Sadly Alex died in 2010 and is greatly missed to this day. Shaman the kinkajou also arrived this year and was often to be seen on a keepers' shoulder around the Zoo.

Alex Oag.

Shaman the kinkajou.

With the tearoom converted to a monkey house with indoor and outdoor areas, it was soon filled with common marmosets, Geoffroy's marmosets, pygmy marmosets and tamarins.

Brown lemurs were next to arrive and whilst they might not have been as colourful (or as loud as the ruffed and the ring-tailed lemurs) they were special and very gentle.

Geoffroy's marmosets.

Brown lemur.

2008

Next to arrive were bat eared foxes, fennec foxes, porcupines, and a peacock whose favourite place was in and around the monkey house! What a character he was, but sadly we found him dead on top of the monkey house in 2012.

Bat eared fox.

Fennec foxes.

Peacock.

Two otters arrived at the Zoo and so the pond became the Otter Pond. Does anyone remember the otter who would stand on top of the bush calling for dinner?

The otters arrive to live in the modified pond.

Along with the otters, fallow deer and Tuesday the cow arrived. These were kept in the area which is currently the car park. Davey, a Shetland pony, joined them and again he is such a well known and much loved character!

Wallabies, prairie dogs and two Scottish wildcats (female and male) arrived from Auchengarrich. Micro pigs also arrived at this time – they were so cute and small – now they are huge!

Prairie dog.

Scottish wildcat.

Micro pigs.

Pygmy goats came from Weatheriggs Animal Rescue and the summer house became their new home. One of them, Bob, was such a character and a favourite with many of our visitors.

Elliott, a giant African spurred tortoise had outgrown his home and his owners donated him to the Zoo. He lived happily amongst several other types of tortoise and the giant continental rabbits, close to the entrance of the Zoo.

The Zoo was delighted by a visit from Michaela Strachan, filming an episode of Zoo Babies. Pictured here with some of the staff, Michaela is holding the two baby skunks that they had been filming, one of them was an albino, hence the names of them Michaela and Strachan! Strachan sadly died in 2016 and Michaela in early 2017.

Pygmy goat.

Giant African spurred tortoise.

The Michaela Strachan visit.

2009

Another welcome addition was a toucan who came from Amazonia and lived in the reptile house. He had a damaged beak but was a welcome sight at the ticket desk.

Jacob, a huge pink pig also arrived to take up residence and he was indeed a character!

Sadly, the reality was that the Zoo was struggling and despite Brian and Shirley's constant injections of cash to keep the Zoo going through the winter, a crisis meeting was called in January to discuss ways of saving the Zoo. At this point they re-mortgaged their home to raise much needed funds for the on-going upkeep of the animals.

Toucan.

Many new supporters came forward and thanks to their help and with various fund raising events, the Zoo struggled on through the year. One supporter in particular must be mentioned – Eileen Boyle, who has been an amazing help over the years in all sorts of ways and still does so much for the Zoo – thank you Eileen.

2013

Having heard about the successful re-homing of the circus bears, Gentleshaws Animal Sanctuary contacted the Zoo asking about the possibility of re-homing a single male lynx. They had cared for him and his father for many years but the enclosure was small and no one else wanted Buster as he had deformed ears as a result of having several ear infections when he was young. Buster arrived in January 2013 and not long after was joined by Chloe, an old female lynx, off show at another Zoo. Lynx are solitary animals, normally only looking for company during mating season, but Buster and Chloe mixed well.

The raccoons moved to make way for the lynx, with new enclosures for them, the skunks and the coati.

Buster. *Chloe.*

During the Easter holidays the Zoo enjoyed a record number of visitors; everyone was delighted with the new look reptile house and other improvements and enjoyed 2 weeks of great weather.

However, during the early hours of Sunday 14th April, Shirley and Brian were woken by the sound of an alarm and looking out their front window, were horrified to see that the Reptile House was on fire.

Blaze discovered.

Within 10 minutes the Fire Brigade had arrived on site and for the next few hours, battled to control and put out the flames. Nothing could be saved of the Reptile House, but thanks to the quick response of the fire fighters, the rest of the Zoo and the indoor soft play and outdoor castle play areas were saved.

Described as "our worst nightmare" the reality of the fire was that it had destroyed 48 species of reptiles and small mammals from the reptile house, together with 11 meerkats and a male otter that had been housed close by. Amazingly, despite their enclosure burning to the ground, the two crocodiles sunk to the bottom of their pond in a "comatose state" and were pulled out by Graeme, one of Shirley and Brian's sons – alive!

Some of the twisted remains.

Fire investigators before demolition.

Thrust into the limelight, the Zoo featured on the front page of all the national newspapers, it really was a terrible time for everyone. Fire investigators sifted through the rubble to find the cause – negligence and malicious intent were ruled out and it was put down to a 'tragic accident'.
The Emergency Services were amazing and we are so grateful to them for their fast response.

In the aftermath of the fire, it was the amazing support and encouragement from public, both in Scotland, the UK and indeed from all around the world, that kept Shirley, Brian and all the staff going through this horrendous period.

Donations started pouring in and within a matter of months, a staggering £110K had been donated to help with the rebuild of the reptile house and other areas of the Zoo.

The Zoo re-opened free of charge to the public the following weekend, by which time a memorial garden dedicated to all the animals that had perished had been laid out with a picture of each species lost. This can still be seen today as you enter the Zoo from the ticket desk, they may be gone but they will never be forgotten. Demolition of the reptile house began the following week.

The memorial garden.  *Demolition begins.*

The two surviving meerkats were treated for their burns and by May were back out in their enclosure. By November they delighted everyone with 2 new pups; a sure sign that they had recovered, felt secure and settled enough to breed – the meerkat family were starting to grow again!

Despite horrendous burns on her tail and each of her paws, the female otter survived and again, was back out in her enclosure in May. A new male was donated from Hoo Farm in Shropshire and the pair seemed to settle well together.

The two crocodiles were housed in a temporary pond waiting for a new reptile house being built.

The two new meerkat pups.  *Crocodiles in their temporary pond.*

In the coming weeks and months, plans were finalised and a series of improvements began with the aim of creating larger new habitats for a number of existing animals at the Zoo. New walkthrough areas for birds, a petting Zoo and importantly an open "meerkat savannah" enclosure on the footprint of the former reptile house were started.

Work in progress for the new aviary.

Birds in the completed aviary.

Work starts on the meerkat savannah.

The completed meerkat savannah.

Chad, a giant African spurred tortoise arrived to join the meerkats and visitors are always amazed to see him out and about in the warmer weather. The cheeky meerkats were soon enjoying free lifts! Two stunning blue cranes also arrived to create a mixed savannah exhibit.

Chad with the meerkats.

Blue cranes arrive.

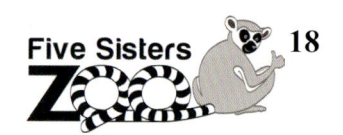

The construction team then turned their efforts to the old monkey house which was demolished to make way for a new improved facility.

The new monkey house under construction.

The new monkey house on completion.

The decision to convert the existing indoor soft play area into a new reptile house was made and the pirate ship was moved to become part of a larger outdoor play area of the Zoo. This came with a promise to construct a completely new indoor play facility at a later date.

Work began to convert the outdoor pirate ship area to a "Petting Zoo" with a medieval theme and this was opened in early December, welcoming Santa in his new Grotto (the Crooked House). Kids especially loved being able to pet the guinea pigs, rabbits and pygmy goats, as well as many other animals living in here, many associated with life in a medieval castle.

Shirley & Brian were asked if they would be able to re-home two young female Arctic wolves from Sosto Zoo in Hungary. These rather timid sisters had been bullied out of their pack and were housed in a small off show concrete hut. Work began to create a new enclosure for them towards the end of the year.

Visitor numbers had fallen drastically this year, as many thought the whole Zoo had burnt down and wasn't open.

2014

In February, staff were delighted with the arrival of 3 otter pups who initially seemed to do well, but sadly one by one they died. Autopsies showed that the female otter had failed to feed and wean them sufficiently due to inexperience – another tragedy for the otter family.

We were also devastated by the sudden death of Goldie our albino Burmese python, she had been at the Zoo for so many years.

The new otter pups.

Our new wallabies.  *The two rhea.*  *Rocky the emu.*

With the closure of Fife Animal Park, the Zoo offered to help by re-homing 9 wallabies, 2 rhea, an emu named Rocky and 2 coati.

By Easter, the majority of work around the Zoo was complete and the feedback from visitors was fantastic! New enclosures for the owls, a play park, a new education centre with a handling room and classroom facility were now all in place. We are passionate about education and believe that we have an important role to connect people with nature. The Zoo is becoming an ever popular destination for school visits, both as a learning experience across many areas of the curriculum, but also as a fun day out at the end of term.

Our new coati.

New play park under construction.  *The education centre.*

Work was well underway with the new wolf enclosure, paperwork was finalised and on the 22nd May, two beautiful Arctic wolves arrived at the Zoo and settled immediately into their new home. Initially very timid, staff worked hard to gain their confidence and a firm favourite with Luna and Aria is Bracken, one of the family's own German shepherds who can sometimes be seen running madly round the outside of their enclosure with the wolves running along with him at the other side of the fence!

Our Arctic wolves, Luna & Aria.

Throughout the year work continued on the new reptile house. It was a huge undertaking and each of the enclosures needed their own humidity and temperature controls, as well as new pools for the reptiles and a new walkthrough rainforest area.

Enclosure Structure.  *Enclosure humidity and temperature system.*

In September, Shirley and Brian received a call from the Belgian Rescue Centre who had cared for the ex-circus bears during 2011, asking if they would be willing to offer a home to 4 ex-circus lions. The answer was "yes" as you can guess, but only if we were able to raise the necessary funds to construct a new 2 acre enclosure and transport them to the Zoo – total estimated cost £150K.

An urgent appeal by the Zoo was launched in October and once again, the public rallied and donations arrived, many fundraising events were organised and word began to spread about the plight of these 4 poor animals.

The lions had been seized from a travelling French Circus in May 2014 by Belgian officials, as Belgian law forbids the use of live animals in circuses. The Circus refused to stop performing or to leave the country, hence the police confiscated the lions and their trailer, driving it straight to the Natuurhulpcentrum who were able to offer immediate sanctuary to them. However, finding a home proved impossible – the lions had no front claws these having been pulled out at a young age and also they had been castrated – hence they have no manes and the appearance of lionesses.

In order to create a suitable area within the existing Zoo, a new area firstly needed to be created for the farm animals; sheep, goats, pigs, ponies and donkeys. This would tie in well with the planned nature trail that would run along the side of the burn already within the Zoo boundary.

Police convoy in Belgium.  *The lions in their temporary home in Belgium.*

On the 30th December 2014 the new reptile house – The Lost Kingdom - was officially opened by Angela Constance MSP. After months of planning and construction work, feedback from visitors was fantastic and everyone at the Zoo was proud to have achieved what they set out to do – to create a facility both as a memorial to the animals lost and do justice to all our supporters who had generously donated to the Zoo following the fire.

This wonderful area is now home to over 40 species of reptiles and small mammals including our two very special crocodiles who survived the fire, American alligators, a leaf-cutter ant colony, monitor lizard, snakes and other species of lizards, pygmy marmosets and Emperor tamarins.

The finishing touches just before opening.

American alligators.

The Lost Kingdom is dedicated to all the animals and reptiles who lost their lives on the 14th of April 2013

The crocodiles are finally re-homed.

Veiled chameleon.

Iguana.

2015

The otters delighted us with 3 new cubs and this time thankfully 2 of them survived and are still with us at this time (September 2017).

Buster the lynx had been under veterinary care since December 2014 showing signs of a cold/infection with a constant runny nose. Having not responded or improved with antibiotics a decision was made to carry out an exploratory op to see what was causing his symptoms. We were all heartbroken when Shirley received a call with the devastating news that Buster had an aggressive tumour in his cheek. Still under anaesthetic they had to decide whether to bring him round and for the next few days/weeks administer high doses of medication or just to let him go and be at peace. For Buster's sake, we had to let him go.

The otters with the new pups.

Poor Chloe was heartbroken and spent the next few weeks wandering round, crying and looking for him. Later that year a new male lynx called Chef arrived from a German Zoo, but Chloe never really bonded as well with Chef as she had with Buster. Sadly Chloe passed away the following year.

Buster. *Chloe.* *Chef.*

Initially it was hoped to bring the lions from the Natuurhulpcentrum in Belgium to the Zoo in March, but we had not reached our target amount to cover the costs of construction of their enclosure, which was only just beginning. You can read the full story of the lions on large boards close to their enclosure.

Two fabulous lar gibbons (otherwise known as whitehanded gibbons) arrived in May. Mo and Ming and their fantastic "call" could soon be heard each day around the Zoo.

Lar gibbon.

Work began on a new nature trail beside the burn, this new walkway would start at the wallaby walkthrough and end at the new area that had been created for the farm animals. This was a huge undertaking, creating many new enclosures and also moving the Zoo boundary fence, but well worth the effort.

In the summer three delightful "elderly" spider monkeys arrived from Dublin Zoo to live out their retirement with us.

After many hurdles, finally in September the lion enclosure was almost complete, the official paperwork in place and the transfer date had been agreed for the 18th October.

Spider monkey.

The lion fund reached £140k and with only £10k to go to meet the target, we were extremely grateful to the Woods Family for so generously donating the last £10k. Shirley and Brian travelled to Belgium to help with the transfer of the lions and on the 19th October everyone got their first view of these amazing creatures. From day one they settled into life at the Zoo and a record number of visitors were recorded that month.

The lions finally arrive.

2016

The new nature trail opened in Spring and added a new dimension to the existing facilities. Sadly the male wildcat died early in January, again from cancer, however after several weeks three new wildcats arrived with us. It was decided then to move the wildcats into a much larger enclosure on the nature trail which had a lot more height and raised platforms.

Muntjac deer.

Wildcat in the nature trail area.

The meerkats once again delighted us with babies in the Spring, their numbers still growing since the fire.

We have been celebrating Stumpy's birthday for many years and this year was no exception especially as he turned 30! We believe him to be the oldest captive living lemur with official paperwork in the UK. Below you can see him celebrating his milestone birthday with his sons. We look forward to celebrating many more birthdays with him!

Work continued with new enclosures on the nature trail and two new species of primate arrived to join the growing family; vervet and De Brazza monkeys, both natives of the African continent.

Meerkats with the new babies.

Stumpy and his sons.

The rest of the lemurs enjoying the party.

At last… work commenced on the long awaited Indoor Soft Play Area. Plans were drawn up and submitted for approval. Once these were agreed the foundations were put in place, followed by the steel framework.

Steel framework in place.

In late summer work began to lay out a new Japanese Garden, the aim of which was to offer a quiet, beautifully landscaped area for peaceful reflection. Initially this was to be completed for Spring 2017, but the Autumn weather was kind to us so work continued at a good pace and we have been delighted with the result.
With the addition of Koi carp into the pond that Spring, we look forward to seeing the garden mature over the next few years.

Excavation work for the Japanese garden.

Central pond in the Japanese garden.

Construction completed.

In October a decision was made to open the Zoo during the evenings in November and December with the whole Zoo decorated with an array of Christmas lights. "Zoo Illuminations" offered visitors the opportunity to see the Zoo in a "different light" and help boost the income during the winter months. This period was therefore extremely busy as thousands and thousands of lights were placed around the Zoo. We welcomed over 11,000 visitors and following the extremely positive feedback we decided to do something similar again in future years.

Christmas lights in the central area.

Aerial view of the Zoo.

In November, we were extremely proud to have been awarded Best Tourism Business Award for 2016 by the West Lothian Chamber of Commerce.

Seen here at the event, Shirley and Brian were presented the award by Nick Williams, General Manager of the Mercure Hotel Livingston. This Black Tie Dinner event, was sponsored by Visit West Lothian and the Mercure Hotel.

Shirley and Brian being presented with the award.

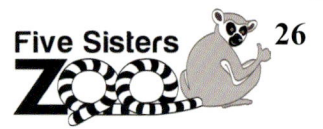

During the Summer the Natuurhulpcentrum in Belgium approached Brian to see if we would be willing to re-home a young male badger. We said yes of course and an enclosure was specially constructed and ready for him arriving. We were delighted to welcome him to the Zoo in November 2016.

You can read Daschie's full story at his enclosure at the start of the nature trail.

Daschie in his new home.

2017

A New Year and a new animal enclosure was ready and so in early February, two stunning young female fishing cats; medium sized wild cats native to Asia, arrived and moved into their fantastic new enclosure (previously the wild cat/the coati enclosure).

The new enclosure for the fishing cats.   *One of the fishing cats.*

Every February the Moffat Centre, the UKs largest University consultancy and research centre for tourism and travel market research, publish their figures. In 2016 the Five Sisters Zoo was rated as number 13 out of the top twenty visitor attractions in Scotland with just over 180,000 visitors. It is also the top tourist attraction in West Lothian.

The new indoor soft play area and restaurant will open early 2018 and this will add to the visitor experience for everyone. We look forward to the coming years; to welcoming both loyal and new supporters to the Zoo and to continue adding to the amazing collection of very special animals.

Ways you can help support the animals:

All profit is injected back into the Zoo to help with the upkeep and veterinary costs, as well as continual improvements and upgrades to the animal enclosures and facilities for our visitors. There are many different ways that you can help ensure the survival of the Zoo :

Simply by visiting - you are helping with the huge cost of running the Zoo.

Spread the word about the Zoo – this way so many more people will discover us and hopefully visit.

Purchase a season pass – they offer great value for money and you can visit 363 days of the year.

Adopt an animal – there are six different options to choose from.

Purchase a personalised plaque – have your own unique message added to a plaque that will be displayed within the Zoo.

Add your name - to one of the many sponsor name boards around the Zoo.

Zoo keeper experience – book in advance to do either a half day for children or a full day for adults.

Corporate passes – these are great for companies/social clubs and enable families to visit all year round.

Corporate sponsorship – we are lucky to have the support of so many local companies. Plaques can be added to any of the enclosures and we are always open to new suggestions of ways of working together.

Volunteering – with a small core staff of keepers, we are always grateful for volunteers able to commit regularly to helping come rain or shine!

Donation tins – there are donation tins around the Zoo and a large coin collector in the Lost Kingdom which is good fun watching the coins roll. All donations go towards the care of our animals and future rescues.

Fund raising – so many people have organised fund raising events for the animals, for which we are extremely grateful. If you would like to arrange an event, please contact the office to find out more.

Facebook and Twitter – keep up to date with what's happening via social media and share with your friends and family.

Trip Advisor – if you have enjoyed your visit share it with others.

Amazon Wish List – details available on our website at www.fivesisterszoo.co.uk

Dear Reader

2017 marked our 12th anniversary and although there have been many ups and downs along the way, we are extremely proud of how the Zoo has developed over this period.

The aim of this book was to tell the story of the Zoo and give you an insight into our journey and the special animals that we have met and cared for along the way. Our passion has always been to offer a permanent home to unwanted animals, many of whom faced uncertain futures. The result has been a very varied and unique collection of characters!

With no external funding we have relied on entrance fees and our own personal commitment to undertake developments, on a couple of occasions we came close to crisis point.

Thanks to the huge support from far and wide the Zoo has grown and flourished, for this we are eternally grateful.

As two of our sons, Graeme and Gary become more involved with the day to day running of the Zoo, we can hopefully start to take life a little easier in the coming years, knowing that the Zoo is safe in their hands.

On behalf of the Curran family, staff and volunteers, we hope you have enjoyed reading our story.

With best wishes
Shirley and Brian Curran

Five Sisters Zoo, Gavieside, West Calder, West Lothian EH55 8PT
Tel: **01506 870000/871111**
bookings@fivesisterszoo.co.uk www.fivesisterszoo.co.uk
Catch up with us on **Facebook** & **Twitter**, or leave a comment on **Trip Advisor**
Registered in Scotland no. SC377723